Remastered

KENNETH KLARNER

eta Publishing

Ocala, FL

Copyright © 2003, 2019 by Kenneth Klarner

All rights reserved. No part of this publication may be reproduced, distributed, or transmitted in any form or by any means, including photocopying, recording, or other electronic or mechanical methods, without the prior written permission of the publisher, except in the case of brief quotations embodied in critical reviews and certain other noncommercial uses permitted by copyright law. For permission requests, write to the publisher, addressed "Attention: Permissions Coordinator," at the address below.

Zeta Publishing, Inc
3850 SE 58th Ave
Ocala, FL 34480
www.zetapublishing.com

Ordering Information:
Quantity sales. Special discounts are available on quantity purchases by corporations, associations, and others. For details, contact the publisher at the address above.
Orders by U.S. trade bookstores and wholesalers. Please contact Zeta Publishing: Tel: (352) 694-2553; Fax: (352) 694-1791 or visit www.zetapublishing.com

First published by Xlibris in 2003
Rev. Date: 2/2019

ISBN: 978-1-7335084-3-8 (sc)
ISBN: 978-1-7335084-2-1 (e)
Library of Congress Control Number: 2018967509

Printed in the United States of America

Introductory Comments

The "Song" of Solomon is a section—really a very small segment—of the Bible that is sometimes called Song of Songs or Canticles. It could not have begun as a song and it was not composed by Solomon—if ever there was a Solomon as described in the Bible's history of the Jewish kings. The Bible's description claims Solomon had 1000 wives, for example.—His "Song" was not about a king who had 1000 wives. At best, assuming "better" is whatever tends to come closest to that 1000 figure, the king's harem in the "song" could have been the 80 woman group that was the total number of wives of king Rehoboam, although we would have to assume there was a confusion of an additional group of wives — 80 — and an original 80 total.—Obviously also disregarding the claim of "virgins without number" is necessary. By the great difference between 60 plus 80 and the 1000 figure we can see we need to look elsewhere than Solomon for the great king involved in this "Song".

Rehoboam is described as the king who was son of Solomon and ruled the Judah part of Solomon's kingdom right after him. He probably could have been confused with Solomon. — "Solomon" also could have been simply a title or a transferable name that kings like Rehoboam were entitled to use, actually derived (probably) from the TEMPLE built by a king remembered only as "Solomon". There is no need to get into the argument about whether there actually was a king Solomon if we are only concerned about the "Song of Solomon" here and consider the source to be something written in the time of Rehoboam.

The following is a reconstruction of the beginning form of this collection of strange declamations that the Bible calls a "song". Actually there is one central story involved that should be considered the source of most of the verses — meaning Bible "verse", plural, here — and other parts are just additions to it. Essentially, the verses are in a DIFFERENT ORDER than they are in as the Bible presents them.

The rendering here into "Acts" is an additional facet of the reconstruction of the ORDER of the parts. To understand the "Song of Solomon" in the Bible you must regard it as a collection of parts that were recompiled in a WRONG ORDER from what they originally were in. Putting the verses and lines in a different order than what the Bible has them is therefore not necessarily putting them in the "wrong order". It may in fact be the right order.

Clearly the "Song" of Solomon is about love. It contains a description of several parts of a spectacularly good looking man's body and also what are apparently supposed to be complimentary descriptions of parts of a woman's body all the way from hair to feet. Privately made copies of a lot of the lines would have likely been circulated among wealthy and educated people and perhaps were sold for interested persons to own.

Before the fall of Jerusalem between 700 B.C. and 580 B.C. there was a time when a wish to revive past greatness must have inspired some of the scholars of Judah to compile the scattered bits of the "Song of Solomon" purely because it was thought to have been written by king Solomon. This compiling may have been done in the time of king Hezekiah, living 100 years before the last part of that period (near 600 B.C.), that would provide a way to explain a strange comparison regarding the chest of a certain "sister" in the Song. — In the last chapter of the Song the sister's chest is compared to either a wall or a door, with remedies suggested for each case. This may be a specially devised message from Jerusalem to her "sister" city Samaria urging it to be a "wall" against the Assyrians. One of the ways for Jerusalem to get a message like that to the potential allies in Samaria when agents of the Assyrian army would have stopped every traveller and prevented obvious encouragement of resistance would have been to incorporate it in harmless seeming cultural works. Once the special extra part was added in, it completed the collection. — It probably was an original unofficial compilation gathered by somebody who afterward provided it to be used for the secret message that was to be hidden in it.

Although the time of the message could be in the late eighth century B.C. — assuming it was the latest time.— If it was intended for Samaria, the other parts of the compilation would certainly be even older. Those parts are the TRUE "Song" of Solomon. By this reconstruction of the original...."TRUE"....form, the world hopefully has the proper "Song" of "Solomon". It is a reconstruction called —The Song of Solomon in the "obviously proper" order. Until somebody disproves the claim, hopefully its validity will be accepted as a reasonable possibility.

Topic One — The Garden Orchard/When Winter is Past

Voice 1
> The Garden; the Beloved without her lover

She
> Come, north and south winds. Blow on my garden. . . .

Voice 1
> Lover, awake.

She
> . . . . So that its fragrance may spread abroad to my lover

He
> I will go to my garden, where my beloved dwells in the flower beds....you who dwell in the flower beds...

Voices (voice 2, voice 3) in chorus
> With winds as friends in attendance—

He
> . . . . Let me hear your voice.

She

    The wind blows the fragrance of the garden to you, my lover

Voice 4

    Let the one who loves her come into his garden

He

    I am coming to the garden, my . . . .

Chorus

    My sister

He

    My bride to be.

Voice 4

    Let the lover come down into his garden . . . .

He

    I have come into my garden.

Voice 4

    . . . . and taste its choice fruits.

Chapter / Verse (From Bible "book", Song of Songs, or Song of Solomon. Chapter and Bible verse are separated by a colon.)

4:16   Awake, north wind, and come, south wind! Blow on my garden that its fragrance may spread abroad (See Voice 1 for further line)

8:13   You who dwell in the gardens with friends in attendance, let me hear your voice!

5:1   (beginning of verse) I have come into my garden

---

see page 10

4:16   (Come, south ....) wind! Blow on my garden, that its fragrance may spread abroad. Let my lover come into his garden and taste its choice fruits.

5:1   I have come into my garden, my sister, my bride . . . . (first line of verse)

6:2   My lover has gone down to his garden, ...

Page 13 source verses.

She

> My lover has gone into the garden, to the beds of spices, to browse in the gardens and to gather lilies. I am my lover's and he is mine. . . .he that browses among the lilies (—is mine—).

Voice 5

> I have gathered my myrrh, (. . . o . . .) . . .

Voice 6

> my spice.

Voice 5

> I have eaten my honeycomb, . . .

Voice 6

> My honey.

Voice 5

> I have drunk my wine, ...

Voice 6

> My milk.

He

> You have stolen my heart, culprit, so be my bride. You have stolen my heart with one glance of your eyes, with one jewel of your necklace.

Voice 6

> I liken you, my darling, to a mare harnessed to one of the chariots of Pharaoh,

Chorus

> . . . . So controlled . . . .

6:2,3   My lover has gone down to his garden, to the beds of spices, to browse in the gardens and to gather lilies. I am my lover's and my lover is mine. He browses among the lilies.

5:1   I have come into my garden, my sister, my bride. I have gathered my myrrh with my spice. I have eaten my honeycomb and my honey. I have drunk my wine and my milk. (Eat, o friends, and drink; drink your fill, O lovers.)

4:9   You have stolen my heart, my sister, my bride. You have stolen my heart with one glance of your eyes, with one jewel of your necklace.

1:9   I liken you, my darling, to a mare harnessed to one of the chariots of Pharaoh.

He

> Your lips drip sweetness as the honeycomb, my bride; milk and honey are under your tongue.

Chorus

> How delightful is your love, o sister, o bride! How much more pleasing is your love than wine, and the fragrance of your perfume than any spice!

He

> The fragrance of your garments is as if a garden of Lebanon was locked up in them. your plants include a grove, an orchard of pomegranates with choice fruits, henna and nard, cypress with nard and saffron, cane and cinnamon, every kind of incense tree, myrrh, aloes, and the finest spices. You need a garden fountain, a well of flowing water. . . .

Voice 7

> Streaming down from Lebanon.

4:10 How delightful is your love, my sister, my bride! How much more pleasing is your love than wine, and the fragrance of your perfume than any spice!

4:11 Your lips drop sweetness as the honeycomb, my bride; milk and honey are under your tongue. The fragrance of your garments is like that of Lebanon.

4:13 Your plants are an orchard of pomegranates with choice fruits, with henna and nard,

4:14 nard and saffron, calamus and cinnamon, with every kind of incense tree, with myrrh and aloes and all the finest spices.

4:15 You are (alternative—I am) a garden fountain, a well of flowing water streaming down from Lebanon.

1:2 (last line)—for your love is more delightful than wine.

He

>I descend from the crest of Amana, from the top of Senir, the summit of Hermon, . . .

Voice 7

>From the lions' dens and the mountain haunts of the leopards.

He

>I am from Lebanon, my bride; come with me to Lebanon.

Chorus

>Like an apple tree among the trees of the forest is her lover among young men. She will delight to sit in his shade, and his fruit will be sweet to her taste.

4:8　　Come with me from Lebanon, my bride, come with me from Lebanon. Descend from the crest of Amana, from the top of Senir, the summit of Hermon, from the lions' dens and the mountain haunts of the leopards.

2:3　　Like an apple tree among the trees of the forest is my lover among the young men. I delight to sit in his shade, and his fruit is sweet to my taste.

Topic 2—Doves

Voice 8

> See! The winter is past; the rains are over with and winter weather is gone. Flowers appear on the earth; the season of pruning has come.

He

> Every dove in the clefts of the cliff, in its rock, in the hiding places on the mountainside, show me your form, ... let me hear your voice, for your voice is sweet, ...

Voice 8, with others

> Coo, coo, . . . (the cooing of doves).

He

> and your face is lovely. Winter is past. The season of singing has come.

2:11   See! The winter is past; the rains are over and gone.

2:12   Flowers appear on the earth; the season of singing has come; (alternative : pruning–instead of singing) the cooing of doves is heard in our land.

2:14   My dove in the clefts of the rock, in the hiding places on the mountainside, show me your face (alternative word–form . . . . instead of face), let me hear your voice; for your voice is sweet and your face is lovely.

2:12   (second line) The season of singing has come

Chorus

        The cooing of doves is heard in our land

He

        How beautiful you are, my darling. O how beautiful your eyes are!

She

        How handsome you are, my lover! O how charming!

Chorus

        And our bed is verdant, luxuriant . . . .

2:12   (last line) The cooing of doves is heard in our land.

1:15   How beautiful you are, my darling! Oh, how beautiful! Your eyes are doves.

1:16   How handsome (or fair) you are, my lover! Oh, how charming! And our bed is verdant.

Understanding the books idea; Where to start

What is provided here is a reconstruction of the beginning form of this collection of strange declamations that the Bible calls a "song". Actually there is one central story involved that should be considered the source of most of the verses, where "verses" means the plural of Bible "verse". If you want to skip to "Act 6", it will be presented there as a series of recitations, essentially like a play. The lines however will be from the Song of Solomon. Rather than scenes alone, the different parts will be called "intervals", such as "hour one".

For those not choosing to see the back story first, the past pages have provided two of the "topics", "The Garden" and "Doves". For a more complete list, the two parts of the book are in the page listing.

The Bible verses as actually given in the Canticles (alternative title) chapters (in particular, the "Song" is after Ecclesiastes, which is after Proverbs) are a poorly preserved form of what was originally written. They are in disorder, with even large sections of sentences moved from where they originally belonged to new positions. By "remaster"-ing the whole set of chapters, a logical reconstruction is created.

One original section seems to have been a presentation in the style of a performance. It probably was intended as some kind of re-enactment of a situation that the king had been in, which involved a woman that he intended to become an important part of his harem of "sixty" plus "eighty" women. The harem women themselves probably were the ones reading (saying out loud) the lines, including one woman that played the role of the key woman. Maybe they wrote the lines and put on the performance for themselves. Another woman must have played the role of the owner of a herd of goats, after the woman rejected the king's harem offer, she became the wife of that man.

The "remastered" form here of Song of Solomon is hopefully put back in the form it was intended to be. The author, if he may call himself that, did the work of reconstruction of the order, or recompiling, that has resulted in the main pages here.

Table of Topics/Contents Topics Part I

Introductory Comments. 1

The Garden Orchard 6

Doves 16

Understanding this Book's Idea; Where to Start 20

Table of Topics/Contents Part II

Vineyards and foxes and apples and shady trees. 24

Description of the new bride/Topic 4 32

Roses and lilies and fruit

    and things in bloom-describing the beloved.. 36

Further description 42

Goats 46

Topics for part 3—Vineyards and foxes and apples and shady trees

Voice 9

>Winter is past. The fig tree forms its (early) fruit; the blossoming vines spread their fragrance. Catch for us the foxes, the little . . . foxes . . . . that ruin the vineyards, our vineyards that are in bloom.

She

>Solomon has a vineyard in Baal Hamon; he lets out his vineyard to tenants. Each is to bring for its fruit a thousand shekels of silver. My family also has a vineyard . . . . and we give two hundred shekels to those who tend its fruit. If I could I would give away my part of the vineyard and not have to pay for the tending of its fruit. Yet it has been mine. I should tend its fruit myself and get income from those who want the fruit. I should tend the other fruit of the vineyard too and let my family give the money for that to me.

2:11   first line—See! The winter is past.

2:13   The fig tree forms its early fruit. The blossoming vines spread their fragrance.

2:15   Catch for us the foxes, the little foxes, that ruin the vineyards, our vineyards that are in bloom.

8:11   Solomon had a vineyard in Baal Hamon; he let out his vineyard to tenants. Each was to bring for its fruit a thousand shekels of silver.

8:12   But my own vineyard is mine to give. The thousand shekels are for you Solomon and 200 shekels are for those who tend its fruit.

He

> You who have been dwelling in the garden of fruit and spices, will you show me your beautiful face and neck?

Chorus

> Are your cheeks beautiful with earrings? . . . Your neck with strings of jewels? We will make you bangles (ear rings) of gold, spangles of silver . . . .

He

> . . . . Let me hear your voice!

8:13 (last line) You who dwell in the gardens . . . . (with friends in attendance)

2:14 (third line) show me your face

1:10 Your cheeks are beautiful with earrings, your neck with strings of jewels.

1:11 We will make you earrings of gold (alternative—bangles of gold), studded with silver (or spangles of silver).

2:14 let me hear your voice

She / Voice 10
> Under the apple tree I roused you . . . .

Chorus
> there (where) your mother conceived you

She
> —there (where) she who conceived you (was in labor and) gave you birth. — Place me like a seal over your heart . . . . like a shield over your arm. Like an apple tree among the trees of the forest you are, my lover. I delight to sit in your shade, and your fruit is sweet to my taste.

8:5   Who is this coming up from the desert, leaning on her lover? Under the apple tree I roused you; there your mother conceived you; there she who was in labor gave you birth.

8:6   Place me like a seal over your heart, like a shield over your arm;

2:3   Like an apple tree among the trees of the forest is my lover among the young men. I delight to sit in his shade and his fruit is sweet to my taste.

Chorus

> Love is as strong as death, its jealousy unyielding as the grave. It burns like a blazing fire, like a mighty flame. Many waters cannot quench love, rivers cannot wash it away. If one tried to give all the wealth of his house for love, it would be utterly despised and he would be scorned.

By this reconstruction of the original . . . . "TRUE" form for the "song", the world hopefully has the proper "song" of "Solomon".

8:6   (for) love is as strong as death, its jealousy unyielding as the grave. It burns like a blazing fire, like a mighty flame.

8:7   Many waters cannot quench love, rivers cannot wash it away. If one were to give all the wealth of his house for love, it would be utterly scorned. (Alternative of that is as follows. —Would he be despised?)

Topic 4—Description of the new bride

(Her husband perhaps? The king called Solomon)
Voice 11

> Who is this coming up from the desert in what is like a column of smoke, . . . perfumed with myrrh and incense made from all the spices of the merchant? Look! It is Solomon's carriage-litter (bed), escorted by sixty warriors, the noblest of Israel, all of them wearing the sword, all experienced in battle, each with his sword at his side, prepared for watching over each queen during the . . . .

—Chorus of queens—
> "SSSSH"

—Voice 11—
> . . . . Terrors of the night.

3:6 Who is coming up from the desert like a column of smoke, perfumed with myrrh and incense made from all the spices of the merchant?

3:7 Look! It is Solomon's carriage-escorted by 60 warriors, the noblest of Israel,

3:8 all of them wearing the sword, all experienced in battle, each with his sword at his side, prepared for the terrors of the night.

King Solomon made for himself the carriage litter; he made it of wood from Lebanon. Its posts he made of silver, its base of gold. Its seat was upholstered with wool, its (purple) interior inlaid with leather by the daughters of Jerusalem.

Chorus

> Come out you daughters of Zion, and look at "King Solomon" wearing the crown, the crown with which his mother crowned him on the day of his wedding, the day his heart rejoiced.

He

> You are beautiful, my darling, as Tirzah (or a delight), lovely as Jerusalem, majestic as troops with banners.

3:9 King Solomon made for himself the carriage; he made it of wood from Lebanon.

3:10 Its posts he made of silver, its base of gold. Its seat was upholstered with purple, its interior lovingly inlaid by the daughters of Jerusalem.

3:11 Come out, you daughters of Zion, and look at King Solomon wearing the crown, the crown with which his mother crowned him on the day of his wedding, the day his heart rejoiced.

6:4 You are beautiful, my darling, as Tirzah (or a delight), lovely as Jerusalem, majestic as troops with banners.

More of topic 4
—Roses and Lilies and Fruits and Things in Bloom. . . .
—describing the Beloved
(a setting in the 2900 years ago period)

She

>If you go to the plain of Sharon you may find a rose. If you go to the valley you may find a lily. I am a Shulamite—and from the valleys. I went down to the grove of nut trees to look at the new growth in the valley, to see if the vines had budded . . . .

Chorus (women)

>. . . . and we would see if the pomegranates would be in bloom . . . .

He

>Like a lily . . . .

Chorus

>among the thorns . . . .

He

>is my darling among the maidens.

She

>Before I realized it I was set in the chariot with the prince.

2:1   I am a rose of Sharon, a lily of the valleys.

6:11   I went down to the grove of nut trees to look at the new growth in the valley, to see if the vines had budded or if the pomegranates were in bloom.

2:2   Like a lily among the thorns is my darling among the maidens.

6:12   Before I realized it, my desire set me among the royal chariots of my people.

Chorus (different)

> Come back, come back, o Shulamite, come back, come back, that we may gaze on you:

Chorus

> How beautiful (are) your sandaled feet, o prince's daughter: your graceful legs are like legs of fawns, (or) of a gazelle. They are two twins.
>
> Your sides behind your gown (behind you) are the equal halves of a melon. Your (belted) waist makes your gown like a royal tapestry. Your navel is a rounded goblet (, the kind) that never lacks blended wine. Your breasts are twin doves each a jewel the size of (the fruit of) pomegranate. Your neck is like an ivory tower, like the Tower of Lebanon.
>
> Your lips are like (the) scarlet (of a) ribbon; your mouth is lovely. Your nose is the work of a craftsman's hands. The jewels of your eyes are the pools of Heshbon by the gate of Beth Rabbim, looking toward Damascus. Your head crowns you like Mount Carmel—(because) your hair is a mound of wheat, encircled by lilies. The king is held captive by your tresses.

6:13   Come back, come back, o Shulamite, come back, come back, that we may gaze on you.

7:1   (last half) Your graceful legs are like jewels; the work of a craftsman's hands.

7:2   Your navel is a rounded goblet that never lacks blended wine. Your waist is a mound of wheat encircled by lilies.

7:3   Your breasts are like twin fawns, twins of a gazelle.

7:4   Your neck is like an ivory tower. Your eyes are the pools of Heshbon by the gate of Bath Rabbim. Your nose is like the tower of Lebanon looking toward Demascus.

7:5   Your head crowns you like Mount Carmel. Your hair is like royal tapestry; the king is held captive by its tresses.

4:3   Your lips are like a scarlet ribbon; your mouth is lovely. Your temples behind your veil are like the halves of a pomegranate. (6 : 7)

4:5   Your breasts are like two fawns, like twin fawns of a gazelle (that browse among the lilies).

He

> How beautiful you are, and how pleasing, o love, with your delights . . . : Your stature is like that of the palm, and your breasts (are) like its fruit. I said, " I will climb the palm tree (up to the clusters of coconuts); I will take hold of its fruit.

Chorus

> May your fragrance be like clusters of flowers on the vine, your breath like apples, and may your mouth be like the best wine when it flows gently over my lips.

7:6 How beautiful you are and how pleasing, o love, with your delights!

7:7 your stature is like that of the palm, and your breasts like clusters of fruit.

7:8 I said, " I will climb the palm tree; I will take hold of its fruit." May your breasts be like the clusters of the vine, the fragrance of your breath like apples, (9) and your mouth like the best wine.

7:9 May the wine go straight to my lover, flowing gently over lips and teeth.

Topic 4—Further Description

He

> My love will be to me a hill . . . . a mountain of myrrh, a hill . . . . a mountain of incense. I will stay through the night on those hills that will be like mountains.

She

> My lover brings me a sachet of myrrh to rest between my breasts. My lover brings me a cluster of henna blossoms. He brings everything there is to be found in the gardens of En-Gedi (the fountain of the goat).

He

> Until the day breaks and the shadows (of night) flee, I will go to each of the mountains of blossoms . . . . each of the hills of incense. You are beautiful, my darling, as Tirzah, lovely as Jerusalem, as the majestic banners of troops.

4:6 Until the day breaks and the shadows flee, I will go to the mountain of myrrh and to the hill on incense.

1:13,14 My lover is to me a sachet of myrrh resting between my breasts. My lover is to me a cluster of henna blossoms from the vineyards of En-Gedi.

4:6 (—Until the day breaks and the shadows flee, I will go to the mountain of myrrh and to the hill of incense.)

6:4 You are beautiful, my darling, as Tirzah (or a delight), lovely as Jerusalem, majestic as troops with banners.

He

> How beautiful you are my darling. Your face overwhelms me. : Your eyes are doves. your eyebrow hair is like goat hair in the time of year when goats descend from Mount Gilead. Your teeth are like a flock of sheep just shorn, coming up for the washing. Your temples are lovely. Your lips are lovely. Your neck and shoulders are lovely. There is no flaw in you from your hair to your neck.

Chorus

> Your hair is like a crown, even the crown of David, with 1000 shields hanging (like those in David's Hall of the Forest of Lebanon), all of them shining like shields of warriors. Your neck is like the tower of David, built with elegance.

He

> There is no flaw in you at all. Your two breasts are like two fawns, like twin fawns of a gazelle, or kids of a goat, twin kids. See!— The goats that browse among the lilies.!

6:5   Turn your eyes from me; they overwhelm me. Your hair is like a flock of goats descending from Mount Gilead.

6:6   Your teeth are like a flock coming up from the washing. (like 4 : 2)

4:1   How beautiful you are my darling! Oh, how beautiful! Your eyes behind your veil are doves. Your hair is like a flock of goats descending from Mount Gilead.

4:2   Your teeth are like a flock of sheep just shorn, coming up from the washing. (Each has its twin; not one of them is alone.)

4:3   (or 6 : 7) Your lips are like a scarlet ribbon; your mouth is lovely. Your temples behind your veil are like the halves of a pomegranate.

4:4   Your neck is like the tower of David, built with elegance; on it hang a thousand shields, all of them shields of warriors.

4:5   Your two breasts are like two fawns, like twin fawns of a gazelle that browse among the lilies.

4:7   All beautiful you are, my darling; there is no flaw in you.

Topic 5—Goats

Voice 12   (Woman's part)
Come away, lover, and be like a young stag on the rugged hills.

He   (different man, part of a completely rural pair that turn out to be goats)
How delightful is your love, my sister, my bride; you are a garden locked up, my sister, my bride. You are a spring locked up, a sealed fountain.

She
(second "beloved" . . . the other part of the rural pair)
My lover should be mine, for I am his. He browses among the lilies in the dampness of the night. Until the day breaks, turn, turn, my lover. You might as well play the role of a young stag on the rugged hills.

2:17   (after first two lines) Until the day breaks and the shadows flee, turn, turn, my lover, and be like a gazelle or like a young stag on the rugged hills.

4:10   (first line) How delightful is your love, my sister, my bride;

4:12   You are a garden locked up, my sister, my bride; you are a spring enclosed, a sealed fountain.

2:16   My lover is mine and I am his; he browses among the lilies.

He

> My sister, my darling, my flawless one. My head is drenched with dew, my hair with the dampness of the night. Daughters of Jerusalem, I tell you—and thereby (I tell) the gazelles and the does of the field—: you won't arouse or awaken love until it so desires. I will go leaping and bounding across the mountains and hills, until the day breaks and the shadows of the night flee, for I am done gra— . . . unh . . . . browsing among the lilies.

Chorus

> Where has your lover gone, most beautiful one?

(She)

> Look for him leaping and bounding about in the hills.

Chorus

> Which way did your lover turn, that we may look for him? He should be with you.

5:2	(last four lines) Open to me, my sister, my darling, my dove, my flawless one. My head is drenched with dew. My hair with the dampness of the night.
3:5	Daughters of Jerusalem, I charge you by the gazelles and by the does of the field : Do not arouse or awaken love until it so desires.
2:8	Listen! My lover! Look! Here he comes, leaping across the mountains, bounding over the hills.
2:9	(first line) My lover is like a gazelle or a young stag.

She

> Listen! He will come here when the day breaks and the shadows flee. He is leaping across the mountains, bounding over the hills. My lover is like a young stag buck (to me).

He

> Arise, come with me my darling, my beautiful one; come (away) with me. The beams of our house are (going to be) cedars; our rafters are (going to be) firs.

She

> Take me away with you. Let us hurry!

6:1	Where has your lover gone, most beautiful of women? Which way did your lover turn, that we may look for him with you?
2:8	Listen! My lover! Look! Here he comes, leaping across the mountains, bounding over the hills.
2:9	My lover is like a gazelle or a young stag.
2:10	(after first line) Arise, (come) my darling, my beautiful one, and come with me.
1:17	The beams of our house are cedars; our rafters are firs.
1:4	(first line) Take me away with you. Let us hurry!

Table of Sections/Contents

Act VI—Memories—Remembering a restless night. 54
               (Hour 1, Interval 2...)

Act VII—The night continues 58
               (Interval 6...)

Act VIII—The King, and the woman separated from her lover 68
               (Interval 15...)

Act IX—The King's concern; her . . . . gratitude 72
               (Interval 20)

Act X—I'm done with vineyards now. 78
               (Interval 23...)

Act XI 84
               (Interval 27...The woman has exited.)

Act XII—Epilog 86
               (Interval 30)

Appendix—First 88
               (Two verses of Chapter 6; Three verses of Chapter 8)

Appendix—Second 89
               (Verses 10 to 16 of Chapter 5)

Index—Showing page references in this book 91

"Act" 6, the start has "hour 1 "and the rest has "intervals" 2, 3, and 4, ...continuing on with 5 and so on. The time units are all indefinite.

Hour 1

Act V I
—Memories. . —Remembering a restless night.

She
I slept, but my heart was awake. All night long I looked for the one my heart loves on my bed.

Interval 2

Chorus
May the wine potion go smoothly flowing as a kiss for the lips of sleepers.

Interval 3

She
I belong to my lover, and his desire is for me.

Interval 4
Come, my lover, let us go to the countryside and spend the night in the henna bushes.

5:2   first line—I slept, but my heart was awake.

3:1   All night long I looked for the one my heart loves on my bed.

7:9   (last part) May the wine go straight to my lover, flowing gently over lips and teeth (or lips of sleepers)

7:10 I belong to my lover, and his desire is for me.

7:11 Come, my lover, let us go to the countryside, let us spend the night in the villages (or henna bushes)

Chorus

—Maybe watch a dance—

She

Let us spend the night in the villages and go early to the vineyards. . . .

Chorus

Of the Mahanaim (the two camps)

She

to see if the vines have budded. If the blossoms have opened, ... and if the pomegranates are in bloom, there I will give you my love. The mandrakes send out their fragrance, and at our door is every delicacy, both new and old, that I have ever fixed for you to eat. It is all stored up for you.

Chorus

If the pomegranates are in bloom, there I will give you my love.

6:13   (last line)—as on the dance of the Mahanaim (it means the 2 camps)

7:12   Let us go early to the vineyards to see if the vines have budded, if their blossoms have opened, and if the pomegranates are in bloom,—there I will give you my love

7:13   The mandrakes send out their fragrance, and at our door is every delicacy, both new and old, that I have stored up for you, my lover.

6:11   (last line)—or the pomegranates were in bloom. (see also 7 : 12)

Act VII
   —The night continues—

                                        (Intervals 5 to 14)

She / Interval 5
         Who is this that appears like the dawn . . .

Chorus
         Fair as the moon, bright as the sun, majestic as the stars in procession? . . . .

She / Interval 6
         I see it is bright behind our wall. Listen! My lover is knocking!

Chorus
         Look! There he stands by the wall, gazing through the windows, peering through the lattice.

She
         My lover is still knocking! Must I open for him? I have taken off my robe. Must I put it on again?

Chorus
         I have washed my feet, Must I soil them anew?

6:10   Who is this that appears like the dawn, fair as the moon, bright as the sun, majestic as the stars in procession.?

2:9   (after first line) Look! There he stands behind our wall, gazing through the windows, peering through the lattice.

5:2   (second line) Listen! My lover is knocking.

5:3   I have taken off my robe. Must I put it on again? I have washed my feet. Must I soil them anew?

She

> Listen . . . . My lover thrust his hand through the latch opening; my heart began to pound for him. My heart was awake. All night long I had looked on my bed for the one my heart loves. I looked for him but did not find him. I will get up now.

Interval 7

> I arose to open (the door) for my lover, and my hands dripped with perspiration like myrrh, my fingers (dripped) with flowing myrrh, on the handles of the lock. I opened (the door) for my lover, but he'd left;—my lover was gone. My heart sank at his flight.

Interval 8

> "Open to me". "Arise my darling, my beautiful one; come with me". My heart had gone out to him when he spoke. I looked (around) for him but did not see him. I called to him but he did not answer. I will venture out now and go about the city, through its streets and squares. I will search for the one my heart loves.

5:4	My lover thrust his hand through the latch opening; my heart began to pound for him.
5:2	(—I slept but) my heart was awake.
3:1	All night long on my bed I looked for the one my heart loves; I looked for him but did not find him.
3:2	I will get up now. (start of verse)
5:5	I arose to open for my lover, and my hands dripped with myrrh, my fingers flowing with myrrh, on the handles of the lock.
5:6	(beginning) I opened for my lover, but my lover had left; he was gone. . My heart sank at his flight.
5:2	(includes—) "Open to me"
2:10	(except first line) Arise, my darling, my beautiful one, and come with me. (Also 2 : 13)
5:6	(the rest of it) My heart had gone out to him when he spoke. I looked for him but did not find him. I called him but he did not answer.
3:2	I will get up now and go about the city, through its streets and squares. I will search for the one my heart loves.

Interval 9

    So I looked for him but did not find him.

Interval 10

    The watchmen found me as they made their rounds in the city. I called—Have you seen the one my heart loves?—If you find my lover. . . .

Chorus

    What will we tell him?

She

    Tell him I am faint with love.

Interval 11
Chorus

    Where has your lover gone, most beautiful of women? Which way did your lover turn, that we may look for him with you?

3:2   (last line) So I looked for him but did not find him. (This and further lines are also in 5 : 6)

3:3   The watchmen found me, as they made their rounds in the city.

5:6   I called him . . . .

3:3   Have you seen the one my heart loves?

5:8   (after first line of verse 8) If you find my lover, what will you tell him? Tell him I am faint with love.

6:1   Where has your lover gone, most beautiful of women? Which way did your lover turn, that we may look for him with you?

She / Interval 12

(Once) when I found the one my heart loves I held him and would not let him go until I had brought him to my mother's house, to the house of the one who conceived me, to the very room . . . . I said to him,—The only man I've ever kissed was a brother, nursed at my mother's breasts. If you were only like a brother to me then if I found you outside I would kiss you and say you were a brother and no one would despise me. I want to lead you and bring you to my mother's house—indeed now it is my house, for she who bore me has died.—I want to give you spiced wine to drink, the nectar of my pomegranates. —That's what I said to him, and then I brought him to my house.

3:4   (after first line)—When I found the one my heart loves. I held him and would not let him go till I had brought him to my mother's house, to the room of the one who conceived me.

8:1   If only you were to me like a brother, who was nursed at my mother's breasts! Then, if I found you outside, I would kiss you, and no one would despise me.

8:2   I would lead you and bring you to my mother's house—she who taught me.(alternative—who bore me.) I would give you spiced wine to drink, the nectar of my pomegranates.

Interval 13

> Daughters of Jerusalem, I charge you, look for my lover among the stars just before the day breaks and shadowiness flees. Look for him to appear in the dawn.

Chorus

> How is your beloved better than others, most beautiful of women? How is your beloved better than others, that you charge us so? Fair as the moon? Bright as the sun? Majestic as the stars in procession?

She

> My beloved is mine and I am his. Let him kiss me with the kisses of his mouth!

Interval 14

> Chorus . . . . "Do you . . . .?" AND She . . . . "I"

Chorus AND Woman

> . . . . feel a faint coming on

8:4	(or 5:8) (start of verse) Daughters of Jerusalem, I charge you—
5:9	How is your beloved better than others, most beautiful of women? How is your beloved better than others, that you charge us so?
6:10	(Who is this that appears like the dawn) fair as the moon, bright as the stars in procession?
2:16	My lover is mine and I am his. (first line of verse 16)
1:2	Let him kiss me with the kisses of his mouth. (verse 2's first line)
5:8	I am faint . . . (part of last line)

Act VIII
      —The King, and the woman separated from her lover—

She / Interval 15

    Is it his (HIS) left arm under my head, and is it his (HIS) right arm embracing me? Strengthen me with raisins, refresh me with apples, for I am faint with love.

Chorus

    Who is this coming up in the arms of our master, as if he were her lover?

She / Interval 16

    He has taken me to the banquet hall. While the king was at his table my perfume spread its fragrance. Therefore I have become in his eyes as one bringing contentment.

Chorus

    Eat, o friends, and drink. Drink your fill, o lovers.

8:3   (2 : 6 is the same)—His left arm is under my head, and his right arm embraces me.

8:5   (start of verse) Who is this coming up from the desert, leaning on her lover?

2:4   (first line) He has taken me to the banquet hall.

1:12 While the king was at his table, my perfume spread its fragrance.

8:10 (last two lines) Thus I have become in his eyes as one bringing contentment.

5:1   (last two lines) Eat, o friends, and drink your fill, o lovers.

She / Interval 17
> I slept

Chorus (on behalf of the king)
> Daughters of Jerusalem I charge you,—do not disturb (arouse, or awaken.)

Chorus (or the king)
> All night long she looked for the one her heart loves. The watchmen found her as they made their rounds in the city. They beat her, they bruised her, they took away her cloak, those watchmen of the walls!

She / Interval 18
> The king has brought me into his chambers. His intent toward me is a loving one; . . . his love is a banner over me.

Chorus
> Those watchmen of the walls. . . .

5:2   (start) I slept

2:7   first line : Daughters of Jerusalem I charge you, ... and last two lines : Do not arouse or awaken love until it so desires.

3:1   All night long . . . . (I looked for the one my heart loves.)

5:7   The watchmen found me as they made their rounds in the city. They beat me, they bruised me; they took away my cloak, those watchmen of the walls!

1:4   (second line) The king has brought me into his chambers

2:4   (second line)—and his banner over me is love.

Act IX / Interval 19

        The king's concern; her . . . . gratitude

King

        The watchmen found you?

She

        The watchmen . . . .

King

        They beat you, they bruised you, they took away your cloak?

She

        They . . . .

King

        My dove, my perfect one.

She

        The watchmen . . . . The king has taken me to his chambers.

King

        The watchmen found you . . . .

(She . . . .)

3:3   The watchmen found me as they made their rounds in the city. Have you seen the one my heart loves?

5:7   The watchmen found me as they made their rounds in the city. They beat me; they bruised me; they took away my cloak, those watchmen of the walls!

3:4   Scarcely had I passed them when I found the one my heart loves. I held him and would not let him go till I had brought him to my mother's house, to the room of the one who conceived me.

1:4   The king has taken me to his chambers.

5:2   (Fourth line) My dove, my flawless one.

She

> The watchmen found me. "Have you," I asked them, "seen the one my heart loves?" Scarcely had I passed them when you found me.

(Interval 20)

> If only you were like a brother to me, then I would kiss you like I would kiss a brother and you would not despise me; (but) I belong to my lover and his desire is for me. I will go down to look at the new growth in my part of the vineyard in the valley. My lover may be looking for me there.

3:3   Scarcely had I passed them when you found me

8:1   If only you were to me like a brother, who was nursed at my mother's breasts! Then, if I found you outside, I would kiss you, and no one would despise me.

6:3   I am my lover's and my lover is mine. (He browses among the lilies.)

6:11 I went down to the grove of nut trees to look at the new growth in the valley, to see if the vines had budded.

Chorus

> It is my vineyard, and it is mine to give. I give you my vineyard, o freer (the meaning of Rehoboam) of the people, o Solomon.

She

> I will give you a thousand shekels worth of fruit from my vineyard. I belong to my lover. I am his. Pleasing is the fragrance of your perfumes. Your name is like perfume poured out. No wonder the maidens love you. How right they are to adore you!

Chorus (interval 21)

> We rejoice and delight in you, for your love is more delightful than wine. We will savor your love more than wine.

King (or other commenter)

> When someone gives all the wealth of her house for love, will she be utterly despised?

8:12   (first two lines) But my own vineyard is mine to give, the thousand shekels are for you, o Solomon.

1:3   Pleasing is the fragrance of your perfumes. Your name is like perfume poured out. No wonder the maidens love you!

1:4   We rejoice and delight in you; we will praise your love more than wine. (We will savor your love more than wine.) How right they are to adore you.

8:7   If one were to give all the wealth of his house for love, would he be despised?

Act X
—I'm done with vineyards now—

Interval 23 / She

    Why am I (a) veiled (woman)? Do not stare at me, daughters of Jerusalem. Dark am I, ... (Imitator's voice)—Dark am I, yet lovely,—a darkness like the tents of Kedar.

(She)

    . . . . like the tent curtains of Solomon. I am dark because I am darkened by the sun. My brothers were angry with me and made me take care of the vineyards; my own vineyard I have given up . . . . neglected. —Oh Solomon, when my brothers die, the vineyard will be mine. I am giving you my vineyard then.

Interval 24

    My lover spoke and said to me, "Arise, my darling, my beautiful one, and come with me. See! The winter is past: the rains are over and (rain clouds) have gone away. Flowers appear on the earth; the season of pruning has come. The fig tree forms its early fruit; the blossoming vines spread their fragrance. Arise, come with me."

Interval 25

    Tell me, you whom I love, where you graze your flock and where you rest your sheep at midday. Why shouldn't there be a veiled woman among the flocks of your friends?

1:5   Dark am I, yet lovely, o daughters of Jerusalem. Dark like the tents of Kedar, like the tent curtains of Solomon (alternative to Solomon is Salma).

1:6   Do not stare at me because I am dark, because I am darkened by the sun. My mother's sons were angry with me and made me take care of the vineyards; my own vineyard I have neglected.

8:12 But my own vineyard is mine to give.

He (Interval 26)

> If you do not know, most beautiful of women, follow the tracks of the sheep, (to) the grazing of the young goats, (and) to the tents, the huts, of the shepherds.

She

> We will graze our young goats by the shepherds' huts. Our flocks will follow the tracks of the sheep to where they rest at midday, beside the flocks of our friends . . . . (It will be thus with me and) my lover, my friends, daughters of Jerusalem.

references for interval 23

1:7 note—if a version refers to a woman that "turneth aside", it really is saying the woman wore a veil. Women wore veils to hide their identity or avoid having their face seen. A man might go off to the side of a path, or turn aside, to go to such a woman.

See interval 25 for 1:7

references for interval 24

2:10   My lover spoke and said to me, "Arise, my darling, my beautiful one, and come with me."

2:11   See! The winter is past; the rains are over and gone.

2:12   Flowers appear on the earth; the season of (alternative to singing) pruning has come. (The cooing of doves is heard in our land.)

2:13   The fig tree forms its early fruit; the blossoming vines spread their fragrance. Arise, come my darling, my beautiful one, come away with me.

reference for interval 25

1:7   Tell me, you whom I love, where you graze your flock and where you rest your sheep at midday. Why should I be like a veiled woman beside the flocks of your friends?

references for interval 26

1:8   If you do not know, most beautiful of women, follow the tracks of your sheep and graze your young goats by the tents of the shepherds.

1:7   Tell me, you whom I love, where you graze your flock and where you rest your sheep at midday. Why should I be like a veiled woman beside the flocks of your friends?

Act XI

(Interval 27)

Note: The woman has exited.

Voice, or Chorus

> The winter is past. Come south wind. The fig tree has formed its fruit. There is an apple tree among the trees of the forest. Its fruit is sweet to my taste.

Interval 28

> Come north wind. Snow crowns Mount Carmel. We descend from the crest of Amana, from the top of Senir, the summit of Hermon. Come with me from Lebanon, my bride. Come with me from Lebanon.

Interval 29

> Winter is past again. Come with me to . . . .

The reconstruction of the passing of time here, with snow involved, is one of the few parts of the work not very easily shown to be derived from the preserved text. There is no snow mentioned in 7 : 5 or 4 : 8. Perhaps the lines referring to snow were lost. Snow being on the top of certain Lebanon mountains would represent winter for persons in the area near Jerusalem though.

2:11   first line—See! The winter is past.

4:16   second line—(and) come, south wind!

2:13   first line—The fig tree forms its early fruit.

2:3   first line—Like an apple tree among the trees of the forest . . . .

2:3   last line—(his) fruit is sweet to my taste.

4:16   awake, north wind!

7:5   (Your head) crowns (you like) Mount Carmel.

4:8   ending—Descend from the crest of Amana, from the top of Senir, the summit of Hermon.

4:8   start—Come with me from Lebanon, my bride.

2:11   (again) See! (The) winter is past.

4:8   —Come with me from Lebanon, my bride. (presume an original form with TO Lebanon)

Act XII—Epilog

(Interval 30)

She

> I am my lover's. He and the children are mine. Our children are like a flock of goats descending from Mount Gilead. Each child, each goat kid, has his twin. Not one sister or brother is alone.

Chorus

> Beautiful are the sandaled feet of the prince's granddaughters. Come away, lovers, in pairs. Be each like a gazelle and a young stag on the spice laden mountains.

References for Interval 30

2:16   My lover is mine and I am his.

6:5 or 4:1 (Your hair is) like a flock of goats descending from Mount Gilead.

4:2   (last two lines) Each has its twin; not one of them is alone.

7:1   How beautiful your sandaled feet, o prince's daughter.

Other references for interval 30

8:14   Come away, my lover, and be like a gazelle or like a young stag on the spice laden mountains.

Appendix (First)

6:8   Sixty queens there may be, and eighty concubines, and countless virgins with designation, (usually this is written "virgins with out number")

6:9   but my dove, my perfect one, is unique, the only daughter of her mother, the favorite of the one who bore her. The maidens saw her and called her blessed; The queens and concubines praised her.

8:8   We have a young sister, and her breasts are not yet grown. What shall we do for our sister for the day she is spoken for?

8:9   If she is a wall, we will build towers of silver on her. If she is a door, we will enclose her in panels of cedar.

8:10 I am a wall, and my breasts are like towers.

Appendix (Second)

A description :
Chapter 5, Verse 10
My lover is . . . .

(Note :) The Song of Solomon assumes that the description of the special man, the lover, is spoken by the woman, his beloved. It may really be a man like Abraham's servant describing someone like Isaac to a potential wife, like Rebekah. IT MAY BE a description of Isaac (!) if that is the actual source;—namely it may be the words of Abraham's servant at Bethuel's house describing Isaac to Rebekah and her family. (He would begin . . . "He is . . . .). . . . radiant and . . .

5:10 My lover is radiant and ruddy, outstanding among ten thousand.

5:11 His head is purest gold; his hair is wavy and black as a raven.

5:12 His eyes are like doves by the water streams, washed in milk, mounted like jewels.

Note 5 : 11 luxuriant is alternative to waxy

5:12 or by the water ducts (instead of streams) — and . . . (doves) sitting by swimming pools.

5:13 His cheeks are like beds of spice yielding perfume. His lips are like lilies dripping with moisture (myrrh).

5:14   His arms are rods of gold set with chrysolite. His body is (alternative—his loins are) like polished ivory decorated with sapphires.

5:15   His legs are pillars of marble set in bases of pure gold. His appearance (or the word may mean body) is like Lebanon, choice as its cedars.

5:16   His mouth is sweetness itself; he is altogether lovely. Verse 15 ends with . . . . This is my lover, this is my friend, o daughters of Jerusalem . . . . If this was converted from a man's speech (saying "This is YOUR future lover, this is my friend") to a woman's speech it must have been presumed she was calling the man a lover and also a friend. Why is the term friend used by a woman? It was not originally a woman calling the man a FRIEND. "The original ending might have been "This is my master, this is my friend." —He would have added, "oh, daughter(s?) of . . . ." (of someone). This might have become a regular piece spoken about a bridegroom at a wedding or on other occassions.

Index

verse	Chapter 1 page(s)	Chapter 2 pages(s)
1	title	41
2	17, 71	41
3	81	19, 33, 89
4	55, 75, 77, 81	73, 75
5	83	68
6	83	73
7	85	75
8	87	53, 55
9	15	53, 55, 63
10	31	55, 65, 87
11	31	21, 29, 87, 89
12	73	21, 23, 87
13	47	29, 87, 89
14	47	21, 31
15	23	29
16	23	51, 71, 91
17	55	51

Index, continued

verse	Chapter 3 page(s)	Chapter 4 pages(s)
1	59, 65, 75	49, 91
2	65, 67	49, 91
3	67, 77, 79	43, 49
4	69, 77	49
5	53	43, 49
6	37	47
7	37	49
8	37	19
9	39	15
10	39	17, 51
11	39	17
12		51
13		17
14		17
15		17
16		13, 89

Index, continued

	Chapter 5	**Chapter 6**
verse	page(s)	pages(s)
1	12, 13, 73	55, 67
2	51, 53, 63, 65, 75, 77	13, 15
3	63	15, 79
4	65	39, 47
5	65	49, 91
6	65, 69	49
7	75, 77	49
8	67, 71	92
9	71	92
10	93	63, 71
11	93	41, 61, 79
12	93	41
13	93	43, 61
14	94	
15	94	
16	94	

Index, continued

verse	Chapter 7 page(s)	Chapter 8 pages(s)
1	43, 91	69, 79
2	43	69
3	43	73
4	43	71
5	43, 89	33 (8:4), 73
6	45	33, 35
7	45	35, 81
8	45	92
9	45, 59	92
10	59	73, 92
11	56	29
12	61	29, 81, 83
13	61	12, 31
14		91

www.ingramcontent.com/pod-product-compliance
Lightning Source LLC
Chambersburg PA
CBHW022213090526
44584CB00013BA/837